First Facts®

Primary Source Pro

Research

Primary Source Audio

Speeches, Oral Histories, Music, and More!

by Kelly Boswell

PEBBLE
a capstone imprint

First Facts are published by Pebble
1710 Roe Crest Drive, North Mankato, Minnesota 56003
www.mycapstone.com

Library of Congress Cataloging-in-Publication Data
Library of Congress Cataloging-in-Publication-Data is on file with the Library of Congress.
ISBN 978-1-9771-0288-1 (library binding)
ISBN 978-1-9771-0512-7 (paperback)
ISBN 978-1-9771-0292-8 (ebook pdf)

Editorial Credits
Erika L. Shores, editor; Charmaine Whitman, designer; Jo Miller, media researcher; Laura Manthe, production specialist

Image Credits
Alamy: Olivier Asselin, 13; Getty Images: Interim Archives/Contributor, 21, Lionel Green, 19, Universal History Archive, 5 (top); NASA, Cover (top left), 17; Newscom: akg-images, 10, 15, Reuters/Kevin Lamarque, 9, ZUMA Press/Minneapolis Star Tribune, 7; Shutterstock: Ebtikar, Cover (bottom left), Everett Historical, 8, imtmphoto, Cover (bottom right), Ksander, Cover (top right), wavebreakmedia, 5 (bottom)

Design Elements
Shutterstock: newwllw

Printed and bound in the United States of America.
1869

Table of Contents

What Is Primary Source Audio?

Machines to record words and sounds were invented in the late 1800s. Since then, people have recorded all kinds of things. These recordings are called **primary source audio**. Primary sources help us understand what life was like long ago.

primary source—an original, first-hand account of an event or time period

audio—having to do with sound and the recording of sound

In 1889 a machine called the Edison Phonograph recorded piano music.

A microphone is used to record a singer's voice.

Different Kinds of Primary Source Audio

Speeches, **oral histories,** and interviews are types of primary source audio. If we study these sources carefully, we can learn important information about people and events in the past.

Sometimes, with audio recordings, someone will **transcribe** the words the person says. That way others can read them.

oral history—a recording that contains information about the past by asking people to tell about their personal experiences or memories

transcribe—to record something spoken or played by writing it down

President John F. Kennedy gave this speech in 1961 when he became president.

". . . I do not believe that any of us would exchange places with any other people or any other generation. The energy, the faith, the devotion which we bring to this endeavor will light our country and all who serve it—and the glow from that fire can truly light the world.

And so, my fellow Americans: ask not what your country can do for you—ask what you can do for your country."

If you read the words out loud and listen to them, your reaction might change. Does the message seem more powerful when you read it or when you listen to it?

Music can be a primary source too. Music can tell us what people were thinking or feeling at a particular time in history.

The Star Spangled Banner was written by Francis Scott Key. He wrote the song the morning after the British attacked Fort McHenry. Key saw an American flag still flying over the fort.

Fact

The Star Spangled Banner became the United States' national anthem in 1931. Many artists have recorded the song since then.

This painting shows Francis Scott Key looking at the U.S. flag at Fort McHenry.

Poet Francis Scott Key wrote *The Star Spangled Banner* in 1814.

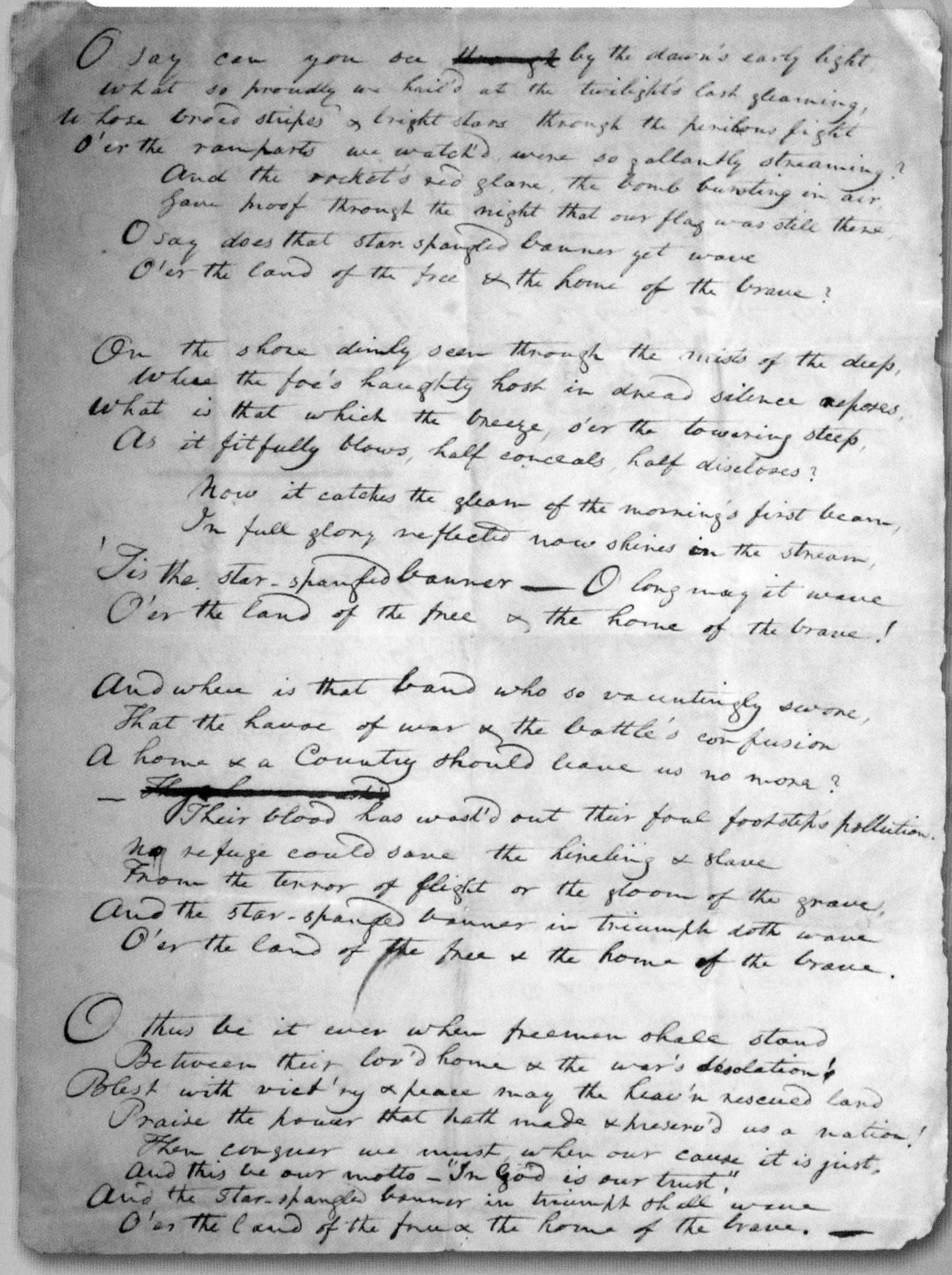

O say can you see by the dawn's early light
What so proudly we hail'd at the twilight's last gleaming,
Whose broad stripes & bright stars through the perilous fight
O'er the ramparts we watch'd, were so gallantly streaming?
And the rocket's red glare, the bomb bursting in air,
Gave proof through the night that our flag was still there,
O say does that star-spangled banner yet wave
O'er the land of the free & the home of the brave?

On the shore dimly seen through the mists of the deep,
Where the foe's haughty host in dread silence reposes,
What is that which the breeze, o'er the towering steep,
As it fitfully blows, half conceals, half discloses?
Now it catches the gleam of the morning's first beam,
In full glory reflected now shines in the stream,
'Tis the star-spangled banner — O long may it wave
O'er the land of the free & the home of the brave!

And where is that band who so vauntingly swore,
That the havoc of war & the battle's confusion
A home & a Country should leave us no more?
Their blood has wash'd out their foul footstep's pollution.
No refuge could save the hireling & slave
From the terror of flight or the gloom of the grave,
And the star-spangled banner in triumph doth wave
O'er the land of the free & the home of the brave.

O thus be it ever when freemen shall stand
Between their lov'd home & the war's desolation!
Blest with vict'ry & peace may the heav'n rescued land
Praise the power that hath made & preserv'd us a nation!
Then conquer we must, when our cause it is just,
And this be our motto — "In God is our trust,"
And the star-spangled banner in triumph shall wave
O'er the land of the free & the home of the brave. —

Listen, Read, Learn, and Wonder

Pay close attention when studying audio sources, like this oral history. If you're listening to the recording, listen more than once. If you're reading a transcript, read it more than once. Can you guess what the person is feeling? What are *you* feeling as you read or listen to the words?

An immigrant family arrives in New York City.

Interviewee: Birgitta Hedman Fichter

Date of Birth: April 7, 1917

Date of Interview: November 29, 1990

Immigrated from Sweden at age 6 in 1924

(Going to School in America):

"I turned seven after we got here and here children were starting at the age of five in kindergarten, so at age seven they put me in the first grade, which was kind of dumb because I didn't know the language and, I didn't know 'yes' and 'no.' . . . I just sat there and every time the teacher even looked at me I would start to cry because I was afraid she was going to say something and I didn't know what, what she was saying. But there was one little girl that I'll never forget . . . this one little girl came and put her arm around my shoulder . . . she just took me outside, stayed with me during recess, and when recess was over she brought me back to my seat in school. . . . I'll never forget her . . ."

This information tells us who is speaking. We learn that Birgitta came to the United States from Sweden in 1924. She was 6. She recorded this oral history 66 years later in 1990.

You can create your own primary source audio. You will learn from people you know.

Using a video recorder or cell phone, interview a grandparent, older neighbor, or a teacher at your school.

Ask the person to tell you what life was like when he or she was young. Ask about important events in history.

These Tips Can Help You!

- Plan ahead! Write down several questions for the person to answer.
- Make sure your recording equipment is ready.
- Begin your recording by saying your name, the name of the person you are interviewing, and today's date.
- Give the person plenty of time to answer each question.
- If you don't understand something, ask the person to explain more.

"Our voices must
be heard!"
LCDB
2012

One way to think about audio primary sources and record our thinking is to answer the "Five W Questions:"

Who?	Who is speaking? To whom is the person speaking?
What?	What is the speaker talking about?
Where?	Where were these words spoken?
When?	When were these words spoken?
Why?	Why do you think the speaker said these things?

When? The words themselves don't tell us when Chief Joseph said these words. From other sources we know that he surrendered in 1877. It must have been in the fall or winter because he's talking about his people being cold.

Who? Chief Joseph is speaking to the U.S. troops that were fighting him and his people.

Where? From these words, we can't tell where they were spoken. We would need to look at other sources to learn more.

This is part of a famous speech made by Chief Joseph, leader of the Nez Percé tribe. He gave this speech as part of his surrender to the U.S. troops in 1877.

"It is cold, and we have no blankets; the little children are freezing to death. My people, some of them, have run away to the hills and have no blankets, no food. No one knows where they are—perhaps freezing to death. I want to have time to look for my children and see how many I can find. Maybe I shall find them among the dead. Hear me, my chiefs. I am tired. My heart is sick and sad. From where the sun now stands, I will fight no more forever."

What? Chief Joseph is surrendering. He doesn't want to fight anymore.

Why? Chief Joseph is tired of fighting and he wants to find his people.

Use the "Five W Questions" to think about this primary source audio.

Who?	Who is speaking? To whom is the person speaking?
What?	What is the speaker talking about?
Where?	Where were these words spoken?
When?	When were these words spoken?
Why?	Why do you think the speaker said these things?

Using Other Sources

You might not be able to answer all of the questions just by listening to or reading an audio source. You might need other sources, such as books or websites, to help you.

This transcript is from a recording in 1969. We read astronaut Neil Armstrong's words as he steps out of the lunar module (LM) onto the moon.

one of the first footprints on the moon

Armstrong: *I'm at the foot of the ladder. The LM footpads are only depressed in the surface about 1 or 2 inches, although the surface appears to be very, very fine grained, as you get close to it. It's almost like a powder. (The) ground mass is very fine.*

Armstrong: *Okay. I'm going to step off the LM now.* (Long Pause)

Armstrong: *That's one small step for (a) man; one giant leap for mankind.*

Fact

Neil Armstrong and Edwin "Buzz" Aldrin were the first humans to walk on the moon. During their two-hour walk they gathered 50 pounds of moon rocks and dust!

Thinking Beyond Audio Sources

What if you asked five classmates to tell about a class field trip? You would hear five **perspectives**. Each person would share memories important to *him or her.*

The oral histories from Birgitta and Gertrude both give us perspectives about school in a new country. It's helpful to study other perspectives on the same topic.

perspective—a particular way of looking at something or considering something

Interviewee: Gertrude (Gudrun) Hildebrandt Moller

Date of Birth: June 15, 1920

Date of Interview: October 5, 1992

Immigrated from Germany in 1929 at age 9

“. . . first of all, I couldn’t speak a word of English, and I was the only child in the school that couldn’t speak English. And it wasn’t too happy the first couple of years but my mama said, ‘Take heart because some day you’re going to be able to speak two languages and all the ones that were teasing you will speak only one.’ And it was true. She was always right . . .”

This 1935 photograph shows schoolchildren working on a language lesson at a blackboard.

Both Birgitta and Gertrude's families passed through Ellis Island when they arrived in the United States. If we want to know more about what Ellis Island was like in the early 1920s, we can read documents, such as newspapers. Or we can look at photographs taken during this time. Together, these sources help us understand the past.

Fact

From 1892 to 1954, millions of people from other countries came through Ellis Island. They hoped to start a new life in the United States. Gertrude and her family came through Ellis Island in 1929.

THOMAS C. MILLARD

Glossary

audio—having to do with sound and the recording of sound

oral history—a recording that contains information about the past by asking people to tell about their personal experiences or memories

perspective—a particular way of looking at something or considering something

primary source—an original, first-hand account of an event or time period

transcribe—to record something spoken or played by writing it down

Read More

Barghoorn, Linda. *Be a Speech Detective.* Be a Document Detective. St. Catharines, Ontario, Canada: Crabtree Publishing Company, 2017.

Corey, Shana. *A Time to Act: John F. Kennedy's Big Speech.* New York: NorthSouth, 2017.

Keller, Susanna. *What Are Primary Sources?* Let's Find Out! Social Studies Skills. New York: Britannica Educational Publishing, in Association with Rosen Educational Services, 2019.

Internet Sites

Use FactHound to find Internet sites related to this book.

Visit *www.facthound.com*

Just type in 9781977102881 and go.

Critical Thinking Questions

1. What can we learn by listening to several different recordings about the same topic?

2. Why do you think it is important to listen to an audio source more than once?

3. Try recording an interview with your grandparent or an older adult. Find out more about their work, families, or school life from long ago. What can you learn about them from listening carefully to their words?

Index